123 SIMPI

123

SIMPLE RHYMES OF LIFE

Gerald C Pattemore

To

Io

DO ENJOY MY FIRST
ATTEMPT

ALL MY LOVE

GERALD
X

ARTHUR H. STOCKWELL LTD.
Torrs Park   Ilfracombe   Devon
Established 1898
www.ahstockwell.co.uk

ISBN 0 7223 3613-6
Printed in Great Britain by
Arthur H. Stockwell Ltd.
Torrs Park   Ilfracombe
Devon

Contents

My First Book

Often I try, to compose a rhyme
Some days, it's bloody hard
My brain's not really functioning
Those days, my head, is made of lard

I can sit for several hours
Maybe write a single line
By six o'clock, I just give up
Go and fetch a glass of wine

A productive day, I feel so good
The words, flow from my tongue
I'm feeling all alive again
Not to mention, feeling young

So now I've written my first book
But it's not quite printed, yet
I really have, my hopes up high
I must not worry myself, and fret

So if you're sat down reading this
You must be rather thrilled
You'll know by now, that I am glad
That my dream has been fulfilled

Potty

I sits on the ring, at the back
Not always, but frequent, I'm black

I'm up there, day after day
Curious children, get chased away

I be black and filthy, I know
But I'm still put here, on show

My smaller companions get more use than I
I just stare though the window, and up at the sky

But on one occasion, the first of the month
I gets a wipe round, and put at the front

All the veggies go in, I feel all anew
My day's here again, they're all having stew

The Pitman

I step out of the cage, for another long haul
Just yesterday, I was down here before

The day seems so long, as I chip at the sides
The dust in my throat, and the grit in my eyes

The day seems so long, it makes me feel old
It's cold, damp and black, this unending road

It's time for a drink, and maybe a bite
I can't see, if it's white or brown bread tonight

The day seems so long, it's back to the grind
My family's up top, but they're still in my mind

My shift's nearly over, and I will be glad
I love my job really, it isn't that bad

I step back in the cage; I'm feeling quite bright
Soon to the top, that wonderful sunlight

Alone

I'm a spotty little thing, with eyes out on show
It's easy to miss me, wherever you go

I'm shy in the morning; I'm a bit shy at night
As I bathe in the evening, in the glare of moonlight

My legs are quite strong, they help me to dive
As I'm swimming around, I do feel alive

My life is so easy; I can sit here all day
Watching the butterflies, especially in May

My time is now drawing, and I'm growing old
Not many will miss me, cause, I'm only a toad

Death

Death is all around us, everywhere we tread
Death for the sad folk, is the thing to dread

Death now is death, once you're gone you've gone
Death for true believers, is the place where they belong

Death then buried, your spirits been released
Not quite, what you always hear, rest in peace

You're entering the spirit realm, it's joy and happiness
Many angels sharing, their love and peacefulness

Meet up with your family, see your neighbours too
All the non believers, just haven't got a clue

Death is not the end, of the things we've been and done
Death is the beginning, of the things we have to come

The Box

You walk into the room, the tele's a blare
If it's not cartoons, it's something to scare

From day to night, from night to day
It's never turned off, what would Granny say

Something's got to be done; it's just like a stain
If we don't act now, it will damage our brain

We all walk around, with square bloodshot eyes
It not only controls us, it controls all our lives

Evening Guide

I'm gazing to the moon out there
Her beauty glistening out
The dry canals and river beds
Our neighbouring sphere of drought

Past days, it may have had cool springs
That flowed so fresh and pure
Bright green thistles, growing tall
Fluffy heather on the moor

Perhaps the sun, just crept too close
For the moon to stay alive
The pressure on this sad poor sphere
Made her struggle, to survive

So now she has, another task
Controls our bubbling tides
Sends her midnight rays to us
On our dark paths, where she guides

God

Who created God
Mighty and the glorious
Controls all the universe
Always reigns victorious

Is God of blood
Or a flash of light
There in the background
On our darkest night

Was God a tiny sperm
As like you and me
Or just appear, just as large
So incredibly

Who came first
The chicken or the egg
Did God choose to be there
Or was he simply led

Does God have a billion eyes
Or uses angels, by the mass
Could be, a sad old timer
Long white beard, and eye glass

Doesn't matter, where he comes from
God's here for us, right now
Just sat down, an aeon ago
To make that loving vow

Mobile Phone

I walk through the streets, I stay in at home
All I can hear is a mobile phone

I sit on the bus, stand on the train
I look all around; they're at it again

These phones are so busy, can't take any more
They sit there and love it; I think it's a bore

The torture is endless, I think I might break
I'll just have to buy one, or jump in the lake

My Mucky Friend

I have a mucky friend, who never tidies up
She's always in the mire; she's such a mucky pup

She strolls around the field, without a thought or care
I would really truly miss her, if she ever wasn't there

She always gets my back up, not once, but twice a day
She jumps around all muddy, then lies there, in the hay

Her name is mucky Chloe, all she does, is scrape and dig
I wouldn't be without her, cause she's my lucky mucky pig

My Shed

Now I'm retired, I stay in my shed
Reality doesn't enter my head

Switch on the fan, if it's too hot
Light the heater if it's not

Sharpen my tools, make lots of toys
All for the tiny girls and boys

I'll nail in a nail, or screw in a screw
If that doesn't fix it, I'll use lots of glue

I hear the mice, under the floor
That doesn't bother me any more

I'm getting old, and getting thinner
The wife shouts out, it's time for dinner

I'm back in the shed, after my food
Wife's not too happy, she's in a mood

I lie in my chair, have a snooze
Play some Mozart, if I choose

One of these days, I shall be dead
I hope they lay me, in my shed

Cloudy

It's raining again, it's ever so dark
You can't even take, a walk in the park

It's raining again, the heavens are grey
Oh how I wish, for a nice sunny day

It's raining again, the puddles are large
Soon you will need, a horse and a barge

It's raining again, when will it end
It's going to drive me, right round the bend

It's raining again, my brolly is broke
I'm not very happy, this is no joke

It's raining again, I need to go out
I'm low on food, and out of stout

It's stopped raining now, what a surprise
I really can't believe my eyes

Our Church

We visit our church on Sunday
To say a prayer or two
We see lots of people there
And sit in our usual pew

We sing hymns and shout with joy
It's such a lovely feeling
That's why so many people go
Because it's so appealing

The priest reads out the gospel
His name is Father Joe
He teaches about Jesus
Before it's time to go

When we leave, we chat outside
To friends, all sorts of folk
Spiritual feelings are very high
But doesn't stop us, having a joke

Our Birds

My wife feeds the birds in the garden
All sorts of colours and shapes

They feed off the table, and from the tree
It's lovely to watch them, it fills you with glee

They are green and blue and yellow and brown
They're up on the shed, and down on the ground

There are thrushes, doves, robins and wrens
Some, you only see, now and then

Finches, blackbirds eating their bits
Up on the box, two lovely blue tits

They are jumping about, all in a flitter
It's good to hear, their chirping and chitter

She

She has long fair, wavy hair
It flows, right down her back
Eyes of sparkling sapphire
Pupils of satin black

Her sensuous lips are warm and soft
Like cherries from the tree
Skin of silk, as the top of the milk
What a sight to see

Her breasts are proud, like a pale sunrise
Her nipples quite erect
They really open up my eyes
I could sit there and reflect

Her curvaceous shape, echoes all the way
Like dunes upon the beach
I stand back in amazement
I'm just too far, to reach

My Faery Friend

I met a small leprechaun, down near the wood
He gave me a smile, and stood where he stood

He said, want some gold luv, I said, that would be nice
He said, give us your handbag, and I'll fill it twice

He filled it with gold, I said, thanks a lot mate
I've got to be going, or I will be late

Hang on my darling, you can't leave the glade
It's taken me hours, to dig with my spade

What can I give you, that won't come amiss
A smile will do, and a lovely wet kiss

Speed of Life

My son's a rep, he loves his job
Always on the go, hasn't time to comb his hair
To and fro, to and fro

Goes to his first call, grabs an order quick
Rings it in straight away, hasn't time, to get sick
To and fro, to and fro

Off to the next one, must hurry now
Bonus, was mentioned, got to work out how
To and fro, to and fro

We see him for tea; he's got to scoff it down
Got to see the boys at eight, meeting them down town
To and fro, to and fro

Easter

I have a cup and saucer
I've had it for years
My grandson bought it for me
It brought me to tears

He gave it me for Easter
Instead of an egg
I use it in the mornings
And take it up to bed

My grandson comes to see me
Three times every week
He's forty-two on Wednesday
I've baked a cake, for us to eat

I'll sit down at the table
He will make the tea
I'll have my cup and saucer
Cause, it's always there with me

My Friend

I have a friend, who's true to me
I wish, I was true to him
He's there, when I'm blind to see
He guides me, when I sin

I suppose I sin, every day
Too weak, my inadequate mind
I perform good deeds, in my own way
But it's not enough, to be just kind

I have to learn, the way is love
Promise to be more righteous
This unique man is so supreme
That's why they call him Jesus

All Around Us

I gaze upon the evening sky
Its heavenly bodies, drifting by

Interplanetary dust, all colours and shapes
What an amazing sight it makes

Nebula, comets, a solar flare
Just get driven, to stand and stare

Galaxies, some far, some are near
It's getting dark, an eclipse is here

So many marvels, that we can see
All made by God, for you and me

Old Sid

If you've ever heard, about old Sid
You would say, that he's alright
But Sid's moaning in the morning
And gets really worse at night

He groans, if his toast is cold
He moans, if it's too hot
Miserable, if he's got to cook
Grumpy, when he cleans the pots

Sid hates it, when it's raining
Loathes it, on a sunny day
Can't stand it in the garden
Whether it's March, or Saturday

The only time, Sid's happy
Is when Sid's got his pipe
Even then, he's very grumpy
Cause he can never find, a bloody light

The Attic

I climbed up to the attic, a mess there was
Wife shouted, tidy it up, I said why, she said because

Some junk up there, was many years old
I humped it around, cause I've been told

I moved that over there, and this over yonder
My head's in a spin, it does make me ponder

Don't chuck that away, we may need it someday
Just can't move it around, let's throw it away

I said tidy it up, and don't be silly
We'll, I'm packing up now, cause I'm getting chilly

Our Holiday

It has taken us ages, to save for this
Passports are ready, a plane we can't miss

We have our costumes, cameras and shades
Kids loaded up, with their buckets and spades

Soon we'll be there, drinking the wine
Exotic restaurants, where we can dine

Beautiful buildings, sights we shall see
Hot sunny weather, it will be lovely

Before you know it, we'll be back this way
Wind, snow and thunder, here we will stay

Until we save up, enough pennies again
We're going to be stuck, with this terrible rain

Confusion

Went to the pub last Tuesday, me, myself and I
Myself had a Guinness; me had a Scotch, I, an American dry

We had a drink and a few more drinks, it was getting late
I remembered, just in time, all of us had a date

We had to meet by the bus stop, I, myself and me
We were late, guess who was mad, her, miss and she

Where

We have to take, what life throws us
Or that's what people say
Do we make, our own minds up
Is that really the way

Is there a destiny
Or such a thing, as fate
Is this, the garden fence
Or just, the garden gate

Are there many angel's
Or a God up there
You will never know
Until you're called, to where

Trip to the Zoo

We jumped on the bus, to visit the zoo
It took an hour, but it seemed like we flew

We arrived at the entrance, the first thing we saw
A beautifully coloured, flying macaw

On down the way, we saw a giraffe
And a family of monkeys, making us laugh

The reptile house, the snakes, what a scare
Down in the pit, a grizzly bear

There were zebras, camels and flamingos
Elephants, gorillas, baboons and hippos

So much to see, have to make two trips
On our way out, we had hot fish and chips

Our Garden Friends

Down by the shed
We have a little gnome
He's there day and night
To protect our home

His name is Peter Pots
He has a silver spade
Always down there digging
He's created, his own glade

His friends like to call
Often now and then
A dwarf named Herbert
And a pixie named Ben

They are always up to trouble
There's no mistaking that
Forever pinching strawberries
And paint each other's hats

They use our tiny birdbath
To go for a swim
Splash all the water out
Then Ben says, it was him

We love to watch them playing
Sometimes, join their games
We know they're full of mischief
But love them, just the same

Gone Fishing

We went fishing the other day, I and my brother Paul
Swore that on this trip, we would go and catch them all

Eager to set up the tackle, and settle back in our seats
Cast our lines across the way, so we had some drinks and eats

Sat there a while, slow was the pace
Four hours on, all we had was a dace

It was the end of the day, feeling quite ill
Our largest catch, was a big slimy eel

We packed up the kit, and finished our grub
The next port of call, was our local pub

The Hare's Tale

A hare popped out, his hole one day
Sun was up, he was out to play

He ran across the farmer's field
Worked hard all year, to grow his yield

Hare ran towards the carrots first
He ate until his belly burst

He was so fat, he could not move
He laid down in, a hidden groove

Three hours later, he awoke
Then heard the farmer, cough and choke

Up he got, ran like the wind
He knew, if caught, he would be skinned

He sped towards, the cabbage patch
Hare and the farmer, were no match

The farmer saw, some movement there
He knew it was, the large brown hare

Cocked his shotgun, took his aim
This should be, some easy game

Bang! The gun went off, the hare he fell
The farmer gave, a mighty yell

No more crops of mine, you'll take
The hare popped up, my death, I faked

This Person

She is a good friend, the best friend I've had
She's there all the time, it makes me so glad

She won't let me down, when I've done something wrong
She has a soft shoulder, for me to cry on

She slaves hard all day, whether at work, or the home
She never complains, or she never moans

She's a lovely person, with funny old ways
She and I will be here, till the end of our days

She doesn't quarrel, or there's never no strife
This wonderful person, is my beautiful wife

The Boys

I'm out with the boys, for a drink tonight
We're out every Wednesday, no quarrels or fights

We try and track down, a different pub
Experience all kinds, of unusual grub

We've been doing this now, for thirty-four years
We have a laugh and a joke, with never no tears

We have traumas in life, as everyone do
But we're still out on Wednesday, we're never blue

There used to be five of us, but now only four
But as years go on, it will dwindle some more

It's a bloody great atmosphere, they're very good friends
It's sad to say this, but, one day it will end

My Hobby

I often practice sketching, during time I get spare
Some say, it's just rubbish, but I don't really care

I just like charcoal in my hands, nice to feel the vigour
What I really like to draw the best, is the human figure

The shapes and sizes interest me; they all are such a wonder
I just sit there with my easel, never worry if I blunder

I know I'm not the best there is, and won't reach any fame
So what I do with all my work, put each one in a frame

Pip

We have a little dog, we call him silly Pip
We take him to the lake, where he loves to take a dip

He always wants a walk, when we've settled down
But not just to the park, he wants to go to town

When you throw a stick, he's bringing back a stone
He's always eating chocolate, not a juicy bone

He's coloured white and black; he's such a shaggy pup
He scratches at the door, wanting us to open up

Out There

The sky emits, a dazzling light
What is it there, that is so bright

I've never seen that glow before
Something strange that is in store

Some sort of craft, it looks all green
Phenomena, this world, hasn't seen

I feel the power, and the tension
It's certainly not, from this dimension

It's coming close, I feel entombed
I feel shut in, there's not a room

A voice is heard, inside my mind
An experience, yes, of another kind

It's telling me, to come on through
I'm not frightened; it's weird, but new

I float inside, now I'm aglow
The craft ascends, and up we go

To the stars, and further out
I will enjoy this, there's no doubt

Decorating

I painted the kitchen, not long ago
A terrible task, of that I know

Cabinets, cupboards, utensils and chairs
Had to be moved, to get out of my hair

Started to rub, the mess and the dust
Wife not too pleased, she started to cuss

It's all over the lounge, you stupid fool
Get back upstairs, silly old mule

Attacked the undercoat, no dust about
Needed a fag, so I had to go out

I smoke in the garden, that's another tale
Back into the kitchen, oh, well

A few days went by, time now to stop
Downstairs all finished, must start at the top

My Tipple

I'm always eager for my tipple
That would be red wine
I often drink too much, you see
Don't know where, to draw the line

My eyes are always slightly glazed
Every morning, noon and night
Gone past the stage, to stand up straight
Like a bush, that has the blight

I would truly like to give this up
Then the wife, would never nag
But I love this habit dearly
Goes down smoothly, with a fag

I think it's creeeping up on me
Head is always, in the trough
But you have to die of something
It's fags and wine, that'll finish me off

Colletta

My wife was at a funeral, to say goodbye
To a dear friend, she met in her youth
Her name was Colletta, a wonderful girl
Respectable, polite, very spruce

A church loving person, with oh so much faith
If you asked a favour, it was fine
She knew there were angels, in heaven
To carry her soul, before her time

May angels, lead you to the Lord
And to your peaceful rest
May the Lord's face, shine upon you
From then on, you are blessed

She's floating on clouds, at the moment
Looking down on her friends, that she left
She loves being there, with the angels
So it won't be that bad, our own death

Our own death, is our own frontier
But we worry, about the pain
But when we are up there, in heaven
We shall see, Colletta again

Could Be Worse

If one is ill, it may seem bad
There is always someone worse
You think the end is coming
And that, you have been cursed

Whatever dwells, you don't give up
We're not meant to be that weak
You fight it through, regardless
Negativity is bleak

We've got to die of something
Should be glad that you've been here
To see this wonderful world
Before the day, you disappear

If you haven't been and suffered
There would be, no place to go
So look forward, to your next life
Be thankful, what you know

Life is Just a Ripple

You throw a stone, into the lake
What a difference, it could make

You see the ripples, as they glide
Far across, the other side

It's just as life, which way to hop
Jump the ripple, will one stop

You take the shot, best you can make
Only you, made that mistake

You made the choice, right or wrong
Is it there, that you belong

If it's your choice, it may not mend
Wrong things come right, towards the end

Guinness

We're off to Ireland, to visit some friends
Catching, the nine-fifty plane
We will be there, around eleven
It's much quicker, than going by train

Arrive with a Guinness, expecting us
It will certainly, slide down a treat
When we've had, two, three or four pints
Time then, for our friends, and us to meet

We will stagger, around the village
Then start looking, for a pub
Probably end up, in their local
And enjoy, some lovely Irish grub

They are good friends of ours, we shall stay
In their beautiful house, down the road
We'll have a great time, while we are there
Before we start, to grow old

We will return, to these Irish folk
When in Ireland, you're never alone
Have some Guinness, a laugh and a joke
Be sorry again, to leave for home

Rat Race

I've been in the motor trade
For all my working life
Watched the models, come and go
Most of it is full of strife

I have my own small business
We sort out dents and rust
Only Brian and myself
It's always just, the two of us

All the colours are a nightmare
Said Henry Ford, a while back
You can choose any colour
Just as long, as it is black

I think it's time, to pack it in
It's been an occupation
I've decided what to do now
Have a bloody long vacation

My Guardian

I have a guardian angel
He's sent from up above
He has the most exquisite wings
Flies, just like a dove

He carries all my prayers
To the Almighty One
He's always by my side
Even in my doldrums

He watches over me
During day and during night
If evil tries, attacking me
He puts up a good fight

I know I have no worries
He's watching all the time
He's such a good protector
For me, and all of mine

Bygone Days

I wander in the garden
To prune a bush or two
I roll a fag, and light it
To stop me feeling blue

I pull a few old weeds
And turn over the soil
Door on the shed, is creaking
Must go, and get some oil

Time quickly shoots on by
The wife brings out some tea
We sit there on the patio
It's only, her and me

We sit and have a short chat
About the bygone days
As we lay there, on our sun beds
In the heat of summer haze

It's starting to get dark
It's time to go on in
My dearest said, the stars are out
Let's stay and have some gin

Hot Flush

The toilet is whistling, whenever you flush
Not the normal sound, a nice quiet hush

Thought, it was the wife, but apparently not
Have to be fixed, before, she gets too hot

Went to the store, to fetch a new kit
Brought it right back, and it wouldn't fit

What shall we do, I need the loo now
Don't worry my love, I'll show you how

Just cross your legs, and hold on tight
I'll have it fixed, by tomorrow night

Sweet Little Ivy

I've watched the ivy, from the pot
Just three inches, to the top

Five years it's grown, in this clay mould
Green fingers not, I have been told

A sturdy frame was built, a while back
So now, it's overtaken that

A firm pergola, I've erected
Won't be long, before it's rejected

Mind of its own, I begin to fear
It's up and running, to the stratosphere

An ivy, not, it's on the walk
It must be dear, old Jack's beanstalk

Insects

Raindrop on a blade of grass
Shinning with the glare
A butterfly just hovers
Happy is her stare

The grass, then starts to move
Just a spider, on her stroll
A worm pops up, sees this beast
And shoots back down below

A snail is sliding up the pot
Looking for, his midday break
He only finds some leaves though
But wished he found some cake

The ground, then starts to shudder
Gardener's footsteps, drawing near
They all look up, with startled eyes
And soon they disappear

Leprechauns Pray Too

Don't suppose, you've ever wondered
If Leprechauns pray too
It's not a silly question
I'm sure, you'll find, they do

In the woods beneath the ground
Most of them assemble
God knows, they're singing hymns
The ground above, doth tremble

Their prophet, teaches them the word
About the Almighty Lord
Of all his glorious angels
How they strike their heavenly chord

Their tiny wooden altar
Where they worship, now and then
A magical race of beings
Deep inside, their holy glen

So if you're on a Sunday stroll
Then the trees begin to shake
The Leprechauns are singing
Fear not, it's no earthquake

The Lord's Back Yard

The gateway is opened, far out in space
What is there beyond, perhaps a new race

The ship is pulled through, no turning back
I'm proud of my crew, they all have the knack

Three days we journeyed, by our earthly time
Its true measurement, was only one chime

We started to slow down, what wonders await
Now we're approaching, the other star gate

We gazed through the porthole, stars in formation
We're certainly in, a different dimension

Some sort of ceiling. We all just leered
Just focused our eyes, then it disappeared

Strange things were moving, soft lights, quite pale
Almost as entering, a large faery tale

No sign of hostility, we felt at peace
Our spiritual being, was on the increase

What have we discovered, we're all so amazed
Our minds are now open, but our eyes are a-glaze

The bright lights have entered, our ship as we speak
That's wrong, we're outside, feeling quite weak

We look far and wide, what we see is supreme
Will we ever awake, from this unusual dream

A soft voice is heard, you have entered the realm
It was not long ago, I was stood at the helm

You must go on ahead, follow the light
The end you have reached, over, is your flight

We have to return, we're not here to roam
Please, there is no way back, this now is your home

You must be mistaken, you're losing your head
I'm sorry to say this, but all you, are dead

Colour

Life's full of colour, to show you the mood
Sometimes you hate them, just sit there and brood

Often there's many, to make you confused
You get so depressed, and turn to the booze

Very rare is a colour, that sends lots of joy
There's always a catch, and often some ploy

The colours are there, around us to see
You need an escape route, so you can flee

Why life a colour, and not black and white
Always a struggle, nearly always a fight

When your life's over, the colours may join
It starts all again, just by flipping a coin

Space

The end of the sky, where do you think
Cannot see or feel it, but looks as black as ink

Looking down from a star, to this little sphere
Take two large steps, you will find yourself here

It's all an illusion; it's meant to be meant
Look straight into space, that space, is bent

It bends for a reason, the best don't know why
But at the end of the day, it's only the sky

It's only the sky, but it's there for our sake
This could be a dream, and soon you will wake

Maybe reality, a speck or a dot
The day you find out, it may be a shock

Checkmate

I was about to play chess, with this master
I felt nervous, and all of a shake
He looked at me, all superior
He thought, I'd give him an awake

We're now under way, I moved a pawn first
He went straight in, with a knight
I could see the whites of his knuckles
He was obviously in for a fight

The game went on, just a few men left
I'm afraid the majority, he had
I wasn't so reckless and nervous now
He was certainly, just as bad

My demise, was slowly creeping up
He could see I was nearly under
But as he moved, he suddenly sneezed
I noticed, he made a blunder

I could see an opening, for my life
He growled at me, looking odd
So I moved towards the checkmate
I had him the clever sod

Smoking

Why do people smoke the weed
Some say it's just habit
Most of them, might bite their nails
They've just got to have it

We like to frequent restaurants
But everywhere they're smoking
You dig into your main course
Then, we all start choking

Some say, we are trying
To give up this awful weed
But I really don't believe them
Cause it's everything they need

The need is greater than the weed
The weed is greater than the need
They are stuck right in the middle
One day their lungs, will start to bleed

Gravity

You cannot see, or smell this force
No one knows, from which the source

Cannot be measured, by any means
It is so pure, and so pristine

It keeps us safe, on this green earth
Since long ago, afore any birth

God placed it here, to, show he cares
Do we ever thank him, in a prayer

It's in no prayer that I've been taught
Long overdue, perhaps it ought

If one fine day it got misplaced
You'd find yourself, way out in space

So totting up, but please take heed
A powerful force, we really need

Nice Life

I glide above, the hills and trees
Say good morning, to the honeybees

Swoop down fast, towards the stream
A frog pops up, he looks mean

Just a sip, and say goodbye
It's safer up, inside the sky

On I go, towards the church
Where on the steeple, I shall perch

From up here, looking down, I see
All the hustle, it's not for me

Down in the field, I see the herd
I'm really glad, that I'm a bird

Lazy

Didn't want to cook, yesterday
We said we'd have a takeaway

Looked at the menu, what shall we choose
So much there, haven't a clue

There were pizzas, kebabs and nuggets galore
Further on down, there was so much more

Burgers, pitta, chicken and cheese
Couldn't pick a meal, from any of these

I really fancied, a nice Sunday roast
We all ended up, with beans on toast

One Thing Left

The love of my life, is now gone away
We were together, for many a day

We used to have laughs, go for a walk
Sit down for hours, to cuddle and talk

Enjoy our holidays, soak up the sun
We had everything, now I have none

Every day, I just sit there and frown
Why oh why, was Rover put down

He's gone somewhere else, left me in need
There's one thing I have, his soft leather lead

Peace

The world as we know it
Is going to her rest
We're so confused at what to do
We don't know what is best

We squabble and fight; we're full of hate
Making way for the undertaker
Can't go on like this, with no respect
Offending the Almighty maker

Try to study the Bible more
Be good in what we achieve
Find a backbone for ourselves
To worship and believe

The end is written true enough
It will start when God is sure
We have to treat all nations right
Not to be premature

Every race should stand up straight
Every priest there, for our guide
So we are drawn towards the light
And never ever run and hide

We must be guided, or we will sin
That it will be forgotten
We've got no right to interfere
And bring on Armageddon

Retired

Life was so hard, and so full of stress
You sweat all day long, but it's never your best

It's tough when you're young, but when you are old
There's no friendly face, the atmosphere's cold

It's no good wishing, your life away
What else is there, you're scatty and grey

You go to the pub, or visit the dogs
The years are now gone, when you were a cog

You were part of that engine, that kept going on
Those were the days, but those days are gone

You sit by the window, nothing to learn
Got to give way, and give others a turn

Photography

I take lots of photos, many of birds
No, not the feathered type, the others you've heard

It's not the models, with no sign of fat
The plump variety, with plenty of that

They are all so jolly, they're never glum
We have a good laugh, with plenty of fun

All colours and creeds, some wear their boots
The majority just wear, their birthday suits

Bloody Sky

I ride the back, of my dear friend
Off to fight, a bloody war
It sends the shivers, down my spine
They go, right to the core

I turn around, and see my home
Silhouetted, by the sun
It's lying low, the sky is red
I must go on, not turn and run

We soon arrive; it's thick and dark
Just then, an arrow parts my hair
Warriors above, below, are strong
They're flying from, the dragon's lair

I've never seen so many breeds
Some wingspans, are immense
Bodies, are going down so fast
The ground is getting dense

Spears and arrows, slice the air
I catch one in my thigh
A dragon speeds, towards my left
He has an evil eye

The rider grins, with mad intent
I try to pull, my bow
I am so weak and losing blood
He hits my dragon, down we go

We hit the ground, with such a thud
And then it goes all black
Soon after, we are in the clouds
I'm riding on my dragon's back

It seems like we're invisible
We're also glowing white
See many others, drifting on
The beginning, of another flight

Manic

I'm driving along, the road's getting busy
My head's in a spin, I'm going all dizzy

The road used to be clear, on afternoon rides
The trees all a-blow, the birds as they glide

But now it's so manic, not a second to spare
It's all topsy-turvy, not one with a care

It used to be safe, we never had jams
It gives me a migraine, please bring back the trams

Childhood

Always wanted to play the drums
But I was never allowed
My parents always shouted at me
Shut that row, you're much too loud

I had to practice, while they were out
Or go to my neighbour's shed
I needed to be, in a pop group
They thought, I was in the head

Years went by, and I'm grown up
Believe it or not, I'm a dad
I have a son, who wants some drums
I'm a bit jealous, but deep down I'm glad

Questions

Pebbles on the beach are plenty
Such the stars, and human kind
Accomplished this, a great creator
Of an extraordinary mind

Just this sphere, are we alone
The universe, is there an end
No one knows, does someone care
Are we put here, just to tend

Are there planets far away
With wonders, such we share
Do they work the land, and love
If so, can you tell me where

Do they worship, our own God
Or even, do they worship
Perhaps we are the chosen ones
All the others just unfit

Finally, our death will come
Then we shall find out more
Will we enter, in the light
Or down into, the deepest core

Which one it is, is up to you
You're judged, how you exist
If you are faithful to the light
When your chance comes, then you enlist

If you enlist, maybe for good
Your soul becomes, an energy
Then you will see beyond the stars
Questions answered, for you and me

Smile Please

People never smile enough
There must be, too much stress
This world, as we know it
Is not quite, at its best

We need to smile more often
Nine hundred times a day
Don't think you're in the office
Imagine, snoozing, in the hay

You use more muscles, when you frown
So let's stop that right now
If you can't learn to smile
I'll just have to show you how

Cold

Caught in the snow, the other day
Nearly froze my bits away

Struggled along, up to my knees
Must get home, before I freeze

Left the car, along the verge
Battery was down, needed a surge

Miles to go, and getting dark
This is no stroll, in the park

I was shaking, no resistance
Spotted a glow, in the distance

Eventually reached it, this was handy
Come on in, have some brandy

I rang the wife, stayed the night
Good English breakfast, feeling alright

Snow was clearing, I used their phone
The services came, and took me home

New Beginning

In the world, a new beginning has come
His name is Jesus, the wondrous Son

Look around, no need to reach
He's here for us, and here to preach

There is no myth; he's not a ghost
He's coming soon, the Holy Host

The world will change, if you believe
Time is coming, no need to grieve

Suffering will end, illness too
The world will start, again anew

The dark will fade, soon to be bright
Then we can enter, into the light

Incredible

They're in everyone's garden, and live under ground
So very strong, and oh so profound

Out in the sun, sometimes they hide
Don't get too close; they'll bite your backside

Just build all the time, do not spit or poke
They work hard together, not like us folk

If they were criminals, they'd be away all the time
So lovely to watch them, like organized crime

Monuments and caverns, a pleasure to see
Are our skills like theirs, no, not we

If we were half as good, we'd sit there and pant
No, not these little fellows, the incredible ants

Teeth

Has many teeth, a size ten jaw
Stand well back, and look in awe

A scaly tail, that likes to whip
Wilder beasts, have had their chips

The crocodile, likes to feast
This prehistoric, angry beast

Any food, is on their mind
Watch it isn't, your behind

The Bible

The Bible, teaches us the way
Does not exaggerate, in what it says

All predications are true and right
On those principles, we must delight

Knowledge is a must, you see
It's written there, for you and me

Please take time, to read this book
There is no trap; it's not a hook

There's nothing there, that will deceive
It's written there, so we believe

The Bee

So clever, is the honeybee
Looks around until it sees

See the flowers, takes a dive
Fill their sacs, back to the hive

Just to watch them, it's quite funny
Collects the pollen, just for honey

Stock the hive, for their young
The rest is ours, for the tongue

The young grow strong, they begin
To start the process, once again

Going By

So many songs, about the Lord
It must mean something good
Like to think, I'm not all bad
And sing more if I could

I close my eyes, and think of him
And then my mouth goes dry
As soon as I, can reach a note
The song has gone on by

My body now, is shaking
A tear, creeps in my eye
My voice is trying, oh so hard
Again, the song keeps going by

A Breakaway

When we reached Weston, the tide was in
It was an amazing sight
Hasn't been in, for eighty-two years
During the day, or even at night

Stepped onto the balcony, looked at the sky
And it was as black as ink
We booked this holiday weeks ago
We never really stopped to think

Unpacked our case, at a five star hotel
Not many of them, down there
Got changed, and went for a drink
On holiday now, without a care

Too much to drink, the food was great
Enjoyed the week, had a lovely stay
Had several walks, seen the sights
But we were glad, to get away

Gravy

Gravy, that brown stuff in the jug
Why do we always use it
Must be, some sort of drug
We pour it on, the Sunday roast
And even, on our chips
Sometimes, it's very lumpy
And sometimes, really thick
We would, truly miss it
If they took it off the shelf
There would never be a substitute
No matter, what your wealth

War

War had started, a sad affair
Missiles flying through the air

Lots of innocent people die
Many of us would sit and cry

But to no avail, the leaders' strife
Do they care, about, one's life

The world must find, an alterative way
We want the peace, want it to stay

All this death, was not to be
Should live together, yes, you and me

Mother's Day

Mother's Day, was here once more
All dressed up, and out the door

First port of call, Blagdon Lake
Sun was hot, started to bake

Was so bright, made you squint
We're ready, for a nice cool drink

Off we went, to a Tudor pub
Where we ate, some Mother's Day grub

Day was drawing, was fantastic
Then Mother broke, her knicker elastic

Had to laugh, she was hopping around
Then they dropped, right to the ground

Thought she would panic, and start to fret
She tore them off, said, what the heck

Maths

Let's talk about Maths, for a mo
Makes the school kids, run and go

Not a subject of my kind
Never had, that special mind

I could add, sometimes subtract
Then my grey cells, would extract

Decimals, was not my thing
Made my poor head, start to sting

Algebra, it made me cry
But not as bad as multiply

A touch more simple, if you divide
Fractions, made my cells collide

Arithmetic, makes up, our space
Never was the thing, I could embrace

Drifting By

I'm crouched on a hill, watching the sky
See my world, as it drifts on by

My life, a cloud, so white and pure
Or is it black, ready to pour

I have my faults, and many too
Not always pink, but sometimes blue

I strive through life, I really try
Am I a cloud, up in the sky

Thick and fluffy, need to immerse
Before my cloud, starts to disperse

Will it disperse, before my eyes
It's just a rhyme, and maybe lies

Trying

No stopping now, I have to say
To find the lost, show them the way

I'm not a preacher, of any kind
A simple man, of simple mind

I look around, and then I know
To show the sad, which way to go

How to start, I'm not quite sure
Is that the path, maybe, this door

I need some help, from up on high
I just can't sit, and close my eyes

I try to help, all those poor souls
Depends which way, the wind will blow

Say What You Mean

When we open up, our gob
Can make, the other person sob

We never think, we're all too keen
Saying things, we never mean

We never stop, to think it through
It's then too late, to start anew

Our tongue, wears a boxing glove
Always hurt, the one you love

Maybe, we should use a pen
Failing that, you count to ten

Young at Heart

I watch cartoons in the morning
My mates all say I'm mad
But I have to see dear Noddy
Or, all day long, I'll be sad

Dennis the Menace, is really great
Road Runner's, pretty good too
Not too keen, on the modern stuff
And I don't like, Winnie the Pooh

I suppose, I'll grow up one day
Nothing I watch, will amuse
Get wound up and exited
To watch, the six o'clock news

Must Try

I try and lead a wholesome life
Being kind, in that I do
It's hard to fight the evil off
It's always there, to conquer you

Must stare it out, face to face
It's the only way to score
If I can fight it off with love
It won't attack me any more

Love is the only winner here
It protects me all my days
I have to stand, and strive for it
There isn't, any other way

I visit church quite frequently
It's there, I get my strength
I can't go out and buy some love
Love isn't measured, by its length

Storm

Was woken up, this howling wind
Seemed like hell, had just crept in

Windows shaking from their frames
Just as a tiger, is untamed

House was trembling, from the thunder
The bedclothes, I was nearly under

Will I be safe, in my domain
My cottage, down a quiet lane

The door burst open, what a fright
Never experienced, such a night

Tried to find, some safer cover
And hope the storm, would soon be over

It's now all quiet, and so calm
But, I still have, a sweaty palm

Faeries

What beautiful little tiny things
Their sparkling, coloured, fluorescent wings

They playfully dance, all sorts of powers
Down in the nooks, up in the flowers

These petit little beings are jolly and gay
Just like the sun, with its radiant rays

Pixies and elves, all over the glen
You only see them, now and then

Faeries have spells, you don't wish to see
You keep well back, from their secrecy

You will, see them, this is no story
Then you will agree, it's all hunky-dory

Gets Better, Maybe

You'll be sorry, when it's too late
When our friendship turns to hate

However bad it is today
It does get better, so they say

Life's too short, it will enhance
You usually get, a second chance

To care for someone, it's so snug
It's great to give, a hearty hug

It's good that people, care so much
They really love, the human touch

The human touch, is what we lack
I'm afraid not many, have the knack

Faith

I do know how to live
I'm not afraid, to die
I know there's someone up there
No need, for you to cry

It's a thing, down deep inside
It's faith, that puts it there
When or where, it's going to be
I'm not one, that really cares

I have an angel by my side
Who guides me, through my sin
So when my day, does finally come
I know I'll be, up there, with him

My Helicopters

Helicopters, fell from the tree
We called them that, I was young you see

They would embed, in the earth below
Weeks went by, they'd start to grow

A little shoot, would then appear
And it would grow, from year to year

Start growing there, so very high
Way up there, into the sky

The day would come, I'd clench my heart
Helicopter engines, then would start

They start to drop, the blades then spin
Evolution now, takes hold again

Lumberjack

I chop down trees for a living
They call me, a lumberjack
When I begin, to chop one
There is no turning back

The forest, is so sleepy
Until I start my task
When it finally, hits the ground
Sounds like a sonic blast

When I've had enough of this
I sit down for my lunch
But when my strength returns again
I go and make the forest crunch

I know I shouldn't do it
Destroying all their leaves
They're put here on this planet
So we can live and breathe

Birthday Girl

The wife's birthday, was coming soon
What lovely gifts, should I bear
Racked my brain, for many a day
And still, I got nowhere

Typical wife, has everything
Typical husband, hasn't a clue
Flowers, jewellery, what can I find
Time's drawing near, what shall I do

Sexy underwear, crossed my mind
But then, it usually does
The lingerie shop, beckoned me in
I found something, for my love

Not too pleased, with my fruity gift
She looked at me, with hate
What do you think you're doing
You know I'm sixty-eight

Witches

The witch is in her cellar
Deep down beneath the ground
She's down there, pulling mandrakes
Their awful screaming sound

She's making spells and potions
For naughty little children
Eyes, bat wings, teeth and tails
She stirs them in her cauldron

Her pointed hat and broomstick
Lay quiet on the shelf
There are many little helpers
Pixies, dwarfs, mischievous elves

Once the potion's finished
No need for her to stay
She would call, her hat and broomstick
Zoom off, up there, away

When she's found her victims
Her spell, she would unfold
She would cast her magic wonders
And turn them into toads

Market Day

It was market day in town
Her indoors, and I went down

She wandered round, had a peep
Over I went, to see the sheep

Meet up later, by the pub
Where we had some market grub

Pies and pasties, it was fine
Especially with a glass of wine

Off we strolled around, like lords
Don't forget my ironing board

Need some nails, for the bench
Don't you want some dog food, wench

We're all done, let's go Dan
So I loaded up the van

Nice day out, again my dear
Shame it's only twice a year

What If

I was watching the sunset disappear
What an astonishing sight
Was as though, the world was ending
And soon, to be permanent night

What if it really happened
We could never live in this place
With earthquakes, and eruptions
The earth would spin into space

It would spin around, the galaxy
Perhaps, find another star
Find ourselves in an orbit
Then wonder where we are

Our neighbours, maybe friendly
Or even, deadly and mean
I was just about to find out
Then I woke up, from my dream

Root of All Evil

That stuff, you always dream about
The stuff, you always need
Yes, it's money, that I talk about
That turns us all to greed

Dad's always there to bail you out
When you're naïve, and young
When you've bought your first car
You wonder what you've done

Then your marriage, comes along
The wife then, takes a turn
Go and find a decent job
Get out, and start to earn

You find a job, it's not too good
Again you've done it wrong
The bills are getting higher
Now the kids, have come along

Crime, must be the answer
Just what, I dread to think
Now I've taxed the bloody car
The tele's on the blink

You wish you were retired
Too far away to mention
More bad news, I've just heard
They're going to stop the pension

You see what life, is all about
We're always at a loss
All the political super rich
Just doesn't give a toss

The Cod Fish

I am a very lonely cod
Swimming here and there
There were, quite a few of us
But now the sea is bare

I loved to swim throughout the sea
Me, with all my sisters
But I am on my own now
They treated them like blisters

We've been fished, by the humans
If like birds, we would be clipped
They've extinguished, all my family
Just to put us, with some chips

My day is drawing closer
Then it will be, too late
Have you heard, the cod's ran out
Never mind, we'll have some skate

Dinosaurs

There used to be some dinosaurs
Spread out from West to East
Some were calm, and ate the leaves
Some were very angry beasts

They roamed the globe, all over
For millions of years
Don't think that we will last that long
There are far too many tears

Can only guess what happened
For them to be extinct
God thought that he would have a change
All he had to do, was blink

He blinked, then the sky turned red
No where to go, they couldn't avoid
Dinosaurs' day, was at an end
God sent, a fiery asteroid

Adam and Eve, then popped their heads
But they didn't do too well
Ate from the tree, of knowledge
Now we're on the road to hell

Antiques

I like to wander round old shops
Looking for a bargain
Wife won't let me spend too much
Must keep below the margin

I'm not one, for dainty china
Can't get my head round that
Unusual things, does it for me
Spring-loaded crutches and top hats

I do enjoy the shiny stuff
Like copper, then there's the brass
I had an African statue once
She had the most delightful ass

I love to visit antique shows
It's a large part of my life
I have many gems already
There's a plus, I have my wife

I have two lovely pistols
Many bayonets on my wall
I've got this rusty blunderbuss
And have two cannonballs

I suppose I'll have to stop one day
Our house has no more space
One way to solve this problem
Must move and find, another place

Crime

Crime today is out of hand
The innocent always suffer
Should speak out more and take a stand
The law must be more tougher

My gran went out the other day
To buy a piece of plaice
Coming home, she was attacked
Several scars, across her face

There is no rhyme nor reason
Why crime, is not attacked
If a vote could stop all this
It surely would be backed

We're threatened in our houses
And driving in our cars
We have to stamp this violence out
Put them, behind the bars

Time

Time has no beginning
It certainly has no end
Something so astonishing
Too much to comprehend

It varies in dimensions
Like worm holes that propel
Unknown, invisible forces
That lie there parallel

You don't know if you're coming
Or just been there and gone
The expanse is so enormous
Can't tell, where you belong

You could start, when you are fifty
Explore for ninety years
Return four hours later
A toddler, full of tears

God has made this wonder
This panoramic aperture
Just to keep us on our toes
So he can shape the future

So don't take time for granted
I know it's weird and deep
As long as an eternity
Or perhaps, a single bleep

Maybe a super bubble
That eventually goes pop
To struggle, is so useless
Too late, you've had your lot

Placing a Bet

There's often trouble, in our life today
We're always at each other's throats
We never learn, from our careless ways
It's like placing a bet, on the Tote

The trouble with bets, there's rarely a win
I suppose people's lives, are like that
But you have to be strong, keep going on
Try to stop, your life going flat

Love, must be the answer, to allsorts
Of problems, we have through our life
If we look up, and trust in the Lord
You'll stop walking, the edge of a knife

Believe me, I'm not telling porkies
I've had trouble in my life, as well
But I pray to our Lord, very frequent
Now my life, is not, one long hell!

Soft Days

Dawn chorus, and the earth awakes
Undergrowth moving, just a shrew
Vines straighten, to meet the light
Everything now, so moist with dew

Sky is clear and so azure
Mountain streams, so fresh and soft
Deep green valleys, down below
Buzzards swooping, there aloft

Daisy seeds, picked by the wind
River flowing, swift and deep
A hedgehog takes her morning stroll
Along the bank, kingfishers reap

The sun is setting, sky so red
World prepares to sleep once more
Insects creep, back to their homes
Make their beds, for this night's snore

Evening comes, the dusk creeps in
Birds are singing, their good night
A dazzling graceful silver moon
Shining down, rays of delight

Suckered In

The enemy's power is growing
Do we have the strength to repel
The evil, is so suffocating
Must destroy, this unholy smell

Down there in Hades, he's scheming
For the chaos, he can cause up above
But we're up here, to surprise him
The ammunition we have, is called love

There's plenty of love, for our purpose
But the weak, has been suckered in
Not sure which way they are going
Evil's got, all their heads in a spin

We're doing our best, to guide them
But some, just don't seem to care
So tied up, with their selfish ways
Not bothered, to kneel down for a prayer

They have to sort out, their problems
Or the future for them, is so grim
They're being picked off, one by one
Everyone, is another victim

For the righteous, the sun now is rising
The fragrance of love in the air
There is no doubt nor bewilderment
Certainly won't, be caught in a snare

Very Soon

It makes us ache, when loved ones die
There is no rhyme, nor reason
Especially when, they are so young
They've not caressed, their season

It began way back, when Adam sinned
He brought death, to human kind
He disobeyed God's wishes
God's wrath, he had to find

It could have been so different
If he never ate the fruit
The pain suffering and sadness
Goes back, right to the root

So don't blame God, when your love dies
Keep your faith, keep it strong
You'll see your loved ones, very soon
I think it's there, that we belong

Day After Day

I lay in bed thinking, what should I write
I look through the window, it's not very bright

The wife says, get up, make me some tea
Before you go down, switch on the TV

I pick up the mail, as I go through the hall
Looks like all bills, not exciting at all

I get ready for work, I warm up the car
I like what I do; it's not very far

The day's nearly over, I'm out of the rain
It won't be to long, before I'm in bed again

Jack

Jack is our budgie, he lives in our house
He's blue green and yellow, and as small as a mouse

He's such a fast flyer, that's why he's so lean
As he skids through the air, he's a flying machine

Some days he's mopey
Some days he's glad
Some days he's dopey
But he's never bad

We love him so dearly; we will miss him some day
We must shut the windows, or, he'll be off and away

Ourselves

How deep is the mind
How deep is the soul
How deep is the heart
I'll just let you know

The mind is so complex
We've used only, one part
Like a mysterious map
We're unable to chart

It's our concentration
Can focus desires
All our mental faculties
And the need to enquire

The soul is so mighty
Cannot touch or see
When our shell has expired
Only then, it's set free

It's our spiritual need
Divine and emotional
An individual being
Most important, immortal

The heart's always beating
Generating a charge
It's warming and caring
The love is so large

Not just an organ
The centre of thought
Has all the equipment
Which cannot be bought

So now you can see
Not just, flesh and blood
So look, deep down inside
And start forming your bud

The First Thousand Years

Jesus will rule, the first thousand years
Can only imagine, what it shall be like
New scrolls will be opened, to show us the path
They will show us the way, that is right

Not many of us, will be on earth that day
Only the righteous, will stand
The one hundred and forty-four thousand
Helping to guide, at the Lord's right hand

Blue electric currents, will envelop the earth
Worldly goods renewed, to perfection
The evil has gone, peace here at last
There will be no need, for protection

Illness, wars and death are no more
Buildings and temples will rise
We'll start to establish, a pure fresh new earth
And look to our God, in the skies

Ferocious beasts, will not roam this place
They'll be here, but friendly and tame
They may even speak, in our language
And call to us, by our name

Money will not be remembered
You give to your friends, without pay
They'll do a good deed, just for you
It will be such, a glorious day

Imagine a day, without any stress
No fights, no quarrels, no strife
The evil, has long been extinguished
What a beautiful, and peace loving life

Will I be happy, in this perfect realm
Tranquillity rules, all the time
I may never get, this wonderful chance
So the day of my death, may be mine

Lace

Bright stars in the sky, millions up there
So many more, than a full head of hair

If you tried counting, it would bring you to tears
It would really take you, nine thousand years

They glisten and sparkle, they look at us too
But looking back, it's a much better view

Don't prance around, they stay in one place
Map out the sky, like a fine piece of lace

If they were to fall, I don't think they can
It would certainly upset, the great cosmic plan

The Ocean

Every eight seconds, the waves, they hit the beach
Foamy little bubbles, so soft and so petite

Splashes up the shoreline, everyone so neat
Shiny pebbles glistening, as the waves retreat

Retreat to the ocean, where it's blue and deep
Way down near the coral, where the fish can reap

Nice and peaceful down there, makes you want to weep
Unlike up the top here, the ocean never sleeps

Within the Mind

We're sown, on the fabric of time
Where dimensions flicker and fade
Are we in a cosmos, so very deep
Where you just can't walk, only wade

There's a precious jewel in our universe
Some say, it's set in the core
Its size, is so very incredible
Yet it started out, as one spore

Just travelling through, a cosmic prayer
Sounds simple, but oh so complex
The geometry of time, is a symphony
As you glide through the endless vortex

Like a volume of ancient manuscripts
Won't unravel, a true signature
You may never unlock this mystery
So sit back and enjoy, the overture

Dreams

Every night I go to bed
Just to rest, my weary head

I know that I, won't get much peace
It's then the spirit, is unleashed

It puts on me a fearful strain
This dreamy spirit, bugs my brain

Turned upside down and inside out
I wake up nights, I cry and shout

There is no pattern, to these dreams
Spirits are there, controlling schemes

I wake up tired, everyday
Eyes are drawn, my skin is grey

Is there no answer to this mess
Am I to live, a life of stress

Overwhelming

I'm in the theatre, having my op
Then all my lights, go out
In a short while, it's all bright again
But my mind, have been turned about

My body is lying, there on the bed
I've levitated, up from my shell
What sort of dimension is this
Is it heaven, or could it be hell

I hear them talking below me
They're saying, that I've been lost
Urgently trying to revive me
My body, is as cool as the frost

This life form of mine, is now on the move
I'm phasing, straight into a mist
I am now entering, a much brighter glow
If I wanted, I could not resist

The glow is so deep, cooling but warm
So caring and drawing me through
I see many figures, in front of me
Cannot be a dream, it's so true

This feeling is oh so phenomenal
I now know what it's like up above
There's wonderful aura of peacefulness
An overwhelming presence, of Jesus' love

My New Car

Bought a new car, the worst that I've had
I wasn't too pleased, yes, it was that bad

Water came in, all over the seats
If you parked on a hill, it would soak your feet

Gearbox was noisy, a job to get gear
Camshaft was louder, radio, you couldn't hear

On the road, it pulled to one side
That so-called salesman, he must have lied

Doors wouldn't lock, boot stayed ajar
Frightened to drive, you couldn't go far

Nothing is easy, why so hard
I'm off to see, our local scrapyard

My Faithful Shoes

These shoes of mine are wearing thin
The laces frayed and torn
I remember when, they were brand new
My little toe, had one large corn

I put cardboard in the bottom
Because the soles have worn a hole
I really love my dear old shoes
But I'm afraid they'll have to go

I've had them heeled a few times
But thinking now, it's twenty-three
I'll be sad to throw them in the bin
Cause they've really been a part of me

Everywhere I go they're with me
Suppose it's only thirty years
They surely will be broken hearted
Then I'll be full of sorry tears

Shakespear Not

We climbed the hill, so steep upon
The wind stroked her red hair, so fine
My arm outreached, touch me not
Open thy casket, we shall sip of the wine

We sat amidst the buttercups
Petals fragile, the yellow so deep
Claret was poured, her head away turned
Her brow did stoop, started she to weep

What troubles you, my fair bride to be
Again I reached to her, she did me slap
'Tis another, my heart belongs, I love you not
No more can I read, of all this bloody crap

Gone

This dear creature of mine, has gone to her rest
Yesterday, she sighed, her last sad breath

We would venture the meadows, under blue sky
And glide the hedgerows, oh, so high

Not many are blessed, with this lovely dream
Would stop and quench, by the cool flowing stream

She would bow her head, let me polish her horn
Can't except she's not here, my white unicorn

She's gone to a place, it's warm all the time
With the other unicorns, I know she'll be fine

Dad

Dad was a conductor, but not of a band
Just collected the money, out of your hand

Many years, he worked on the bus
I would get a free ride, to the terminus

Was a loving person, this special chap
Proud of his uniform, even his cap

Worked very hard, put food on the table
Watched over us, while he was able

Illness got hold, and then he passed away
I miss him dearly, every day

Gone on ahead, to the warm sunny side
When I see him again, I'll expect a free ride

We'll sit right at the back, only us
And ride on a shiny, golden bus

Cacti

The wife grows cacti, in her spare time
It beats hanging washing, on the line

The greenhouse, summerhouse, all over the place
Would think she started, a new kind of race

They are tall, thin, short and fat
Year after year, that's all she's at

Hardly goes out, no time for a bite
In her gloves, from morning till night

Often at shows, sometimes gets picked
She really loves, these little pricks

Bored

Sat in the garden, a beautiful day
With a cool drink by my side
Dodging the bees, as they hover around
There's not many places to hide

It's all very nice, and tranquil
Sit and hear, the flowers grow
The ants are scurrying all around
The strawberry pot, in full flow

I can't sit here for too long
It's starting to do my head
I'll have to make a move, and start
To paint my sad looking shed

Day Out

Went to Weymouth, on the train
To get away, from all this rain

When we arrived, the sky was blue
There was no damp, not even dew

Feeling peckish, we looked for some food
Found a small café, a little bit crude

Had a wander round, paddled the sea
Life at the moment, was filled with spree

The wife said to me, it's time for the train
I to her, suppose it's back to the rain

Bad Hair Day

Just had my hair done lovely
For a very expensive do
I stepped out of the salon
Then the bloody wind, just blew

I could have cried for ever
That's exactly what I did
A wasteful morning's work
Plus paying forty quid

I then retraced my steps
Had it all done again
The wind had eased up now
It started then to rain

So I ordered up a taxi
Cause I never had a hat
As I opened up the front door
A bloody pigeon did me, splat

Utopia

This strange word, Utopia, means
'The perfect state of things'
Long life, health and happiness
Soft violets in the spring

It could mean so many things
To all sorts of different folk
An evening at the ballet
A nice free-range egg yolk

To see the face of Jesus
Feel his love, so great
To know where you are going
And what would be your fate

It's just like buried treasure
That you can never find
But it's there in the heart
In the soul and in the mind

Secret Lives

I'm sitting in my garden
The air is warm and soft
I sense the faeries hiding
I look, and they're aloft

Up in the trees they dart
Frightened to be seen
I see at least a dozen
They're watching, oh so keen

I whisper, come on down
There's nothing here to fear
They vanish even deeper
Will they ever come so near

A brave one pops her head
The rest have just abscond
She's grasping something shiny
Looks like a magic wand

She's pointing it towards me
Some sparkling dust descends
I'm now four inches high
Will she ever make amends

The leaves then start to quiver
Many heads are popping out
They're laughing there, and shouting
I'm no longer, that large lout

They all gather round to see me
The fear is there no more
A friendly smile I give them
I'm then taken on this tour

The ground then rises up
By magic, who's to know
I'm guided down some wonky steps
Towards a gentle glow

As we descend it brightens
Phosphorous stones to show the way
Am I here for an eternity
Or here for just a day

My Last Day

My last day's arrived, on this pleasant earth
The time is soon, when I start my rebirth

So much to do, with the time that I have
It's speeding along, at the rate of a grav

The first person to see, is my parish priest
Information I need, before I'm deceased

Loved ones to see, before my farewell
No time for the gym, on my barbell

A last look at my Bible, before my demise
The short time I have, I must maximize

I shall take a short walk, collect all my thoughts
Remember the things, of that I've been taught

One thing for sure, at the end of the day
My favourite meal, will be coming my way

I'll start with some soup, as made by my mam
To follow, some vegetables, and tasty roast lamb

There's still much to do, before I have that
Pay all my bills, and that dreaded vat

Won't leave this earth, unless my slate's clean
It must be as though, I've never been

The sun has gone down, I've had my last meal
Feeling quite good, not at all feeling ill

Time to relax now, I'm not in a state
I'll sit for a while, and just meditate

I'll open a bottle, of my finest red wine
And look to the heavens, and wait for the sign

I've had very few grumbles, while I've been here
I just look for the love, not just the fear

I believe he will take me, I hope I'm not wrong
Just have to be patient, and be very strong

I've been quite a good fellow, I'm not all bad
A last sip of wine, and finish my fag

I'm sensing the power, it's all going light
The brightness is . . . .

Just a Few Words

The dove flew in, from yonder cloud
She perched upon my palm
She looked through my eyes, into my soul
That it was not, all calm
She comes with purpose, in her heart
To show the true pathway
Follow the flame, from whence it came
To the light, without an end
Just around the bloody bend
That's all I've got to say

Hope you enjoyed